# Get Whale

## Coloring and Activity Book For Kids

HOPE ewe GET WOOL soon!

HOPE YOU ARE GETTING GREAT

MEDICAL TWEETMENT

HOPE YOU HAVE A GREAT DOGTOR!

HERD YOU WERE udder the WEATHER

HOPE YOU
PEEL
BETTER SOON !

www.riverbreezepress.com

**This book belongs to:**

_____

Why did the cow cross the road?

To get to the udder side.

What do you call an unhappy pea?

Grum-pea.

# Peas GET WELL SOON

What comes down but never goes up?

Rain.

What do dogs have that no
other animal has?

Puppies.

How many months of the
year have 28 days?

All of them.

Why do dogs run in circles?

Because it's hard to run in squares.

# What has a neck but no head?

# Hope EWE GET WOOL soon!

Where do fish keep their money?

In the river bank.

What kind of dog do vampires have?

Bloodhounds.

What are the hardest kind of beans to grow?

Jelly beans.

What is a mouse's favorite game?

Hide and squeak.

Why did the cabbage win the race?

Because it was a head.

Why do bees have sticky hair?

Because they use honey combs.

What is a cat's favorite color?

Purrr-ple.

Why did the tiger always lose
at cards?

Because he was playing with a bunch of cheetahs.

What did the banana say to
the monkey?

Nothing, bananas can't talk.

I HOPE YOU PEEL BETTER SOON

Why did the banana go to the doctor?

It wasn't peeling well.

How do trees get online?

They log in.

Why did the whale cross the road?

To get to the other tide.

What does a duck like with
her soup?

Quackers.

FIND
ONE
OF A KIND

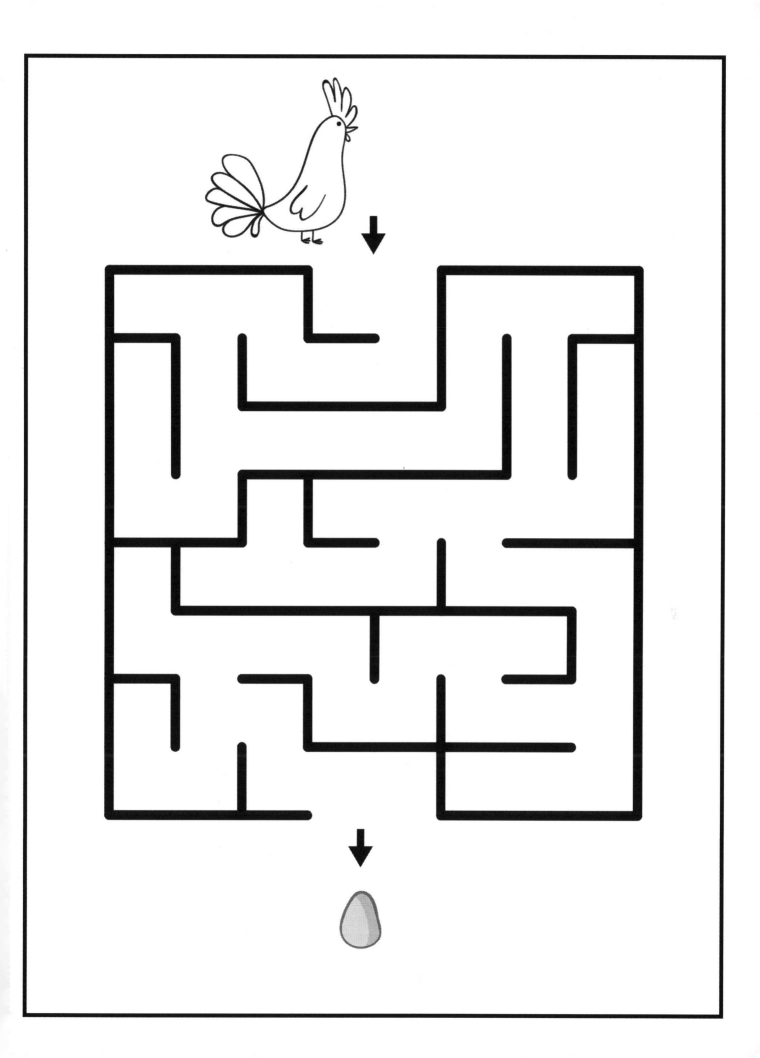

# OCEAN

```
E  Q  Y  Q  F  V  J  K  R  P  K
A  P  C  E  M  F  R  E  J  K  K
G  S  E  O  T  P  D  H  E  P  S
L  R  H  P  N  N  M  A  L  C  T
A  L  L  A  U  C  G  H  L  K  N
L  R  K  O  R  B  H  N  Y  C  E
W  Y  L  K  A  K  L  X  F  O  R
H  F  M  R  P  L  E  K  I  R  R
A  J  C  L  C  D  E  X  S  A  U
L  B  L  O  W  F  I  S  H  L  C
E  S  E  A  L  O  Y  S  T  E  R
```

| algae    | currents  | reef  |
| blowfish | eel       | seal  |
| clam     | flounder  | shark |
| conch    | jellyfish | whale |
| coral    | kelp      |       |
| crab     | oyster    |       |

# PIRATES

```
C E R A H O Y F H K C
H R E A G A L F C O K
E U J N I G K J M O R
S S C T A D C P O M E
T A A R C C A H T T O
G E P R E S I D A H C
B R T O S W L R N B E
R T A H T O I R R J A
C W I C G P R L M U N
H W N N T O R R A P H
C Q V A M U T I N Y P
```

ahoy          hook
anchor        hurricane
captain       mutiny
chest         ocean
compass       parrot
crew          pirate
flag          raid
gold          treasure

Can you find 10 differences?

# Find the ten differences between the two pictures.

# BIRDS

```
F  Z  T  D  E  Y  Z  Z  T  T  R  W  R
B  O  W  L  R  A  X  K  L  R  O  H  O
C  V  Z  A  R  C  G  K  K  R  N  B  O
Z  R  N  R  B  Z  R  L  R  O  R  T  S
F  A  P  M  L  D  T  A  E  Q  O  M  T
C  L  E  R  U  N  P  G  N  R  B  M  E
T  N  A  F  E  S  I  W  R  E  I  P  R
N  S  C  M  B  P  O  A  P  N  N  B  X
S  W  O  Z  I  R  P  E  N  G  U  I  N
T  A  C  P  R  N  N  B  K  X  L  C  F
O  N  K  A  D  H  G  B  F  K  R  N  C
R  P  P  T  B  K  K  O  G  O  O  S  E
K  S  K  R  R  K  F  E  A  T  H  E  R
```

| | | |
|---|---|---|
| bluebird | goose | robin |
| canary | owl | rooster |
| crane | parrot | sparrow |
| eagle | peacock | sparrow |
| feather | penguin | stork |
| flamingo | pigeon | swan |

# CASTLES

```
T  H  C  D  R  K  I  N  G
F  Z  K  E  R  N  G  K  Q
O  P  W  I  W  A  T  Y  U
R  O  J  O  N  A  G  T  E
T  D  R  K  O  G  V  O  E
M  C  X  M  D  C  D  C  N
C  J  E  W  E  L  S  O  T
Q  P  R  I  N  C  E  M  M
N  P  R  I  N  C  E  S  S
```

| crown | king | princess |
|---|---|---|
| dragon | kingdom | queen |
| fort | moat | tower |
| jewels | prince | |

# CATS

```
L  Y  T  H  D  K  L  P  W  G  M
D  I  H  B  C  E  E  A  I  K  W
H  C  O  R  C  P  O  N  L  I  W
T  G  A  N  T  N  P  T  D  T  G
T  N  U  L  R  Y  A  H  C  T  L
V  O  G  E  I  D  R  E  A  E  B
P  Q  G  K  G  C  D  R  T  N  Y
K  I  N  V  C  D  O  Q  K  E  N
T  B  M  R  L  Y  N  X  L  L  C
Z  L  P  U  M  A  K  L  K  H  N
R  C  H  E  E  T  A  H  V  J  Q
```

| | | |
|---|---|---|
| alley | leopard | pounce |
| calico | lion | puma |
| cheetah | lynx | tiger |
| kitten | panther | wildcat |

# COLORS

```
G B L U E E R O W
R C R G L W L R H
E K H P O D H A I
E B R L N N L N T
N U L W P Q D G E
P E O A Z I R E D
Y R K V C W N L T
B T T M T K K K J
Z T T V I O L E T
```

| black | orange | violet |
| blue | pink | white |
| brown | purple | yellow |
| green | red | |

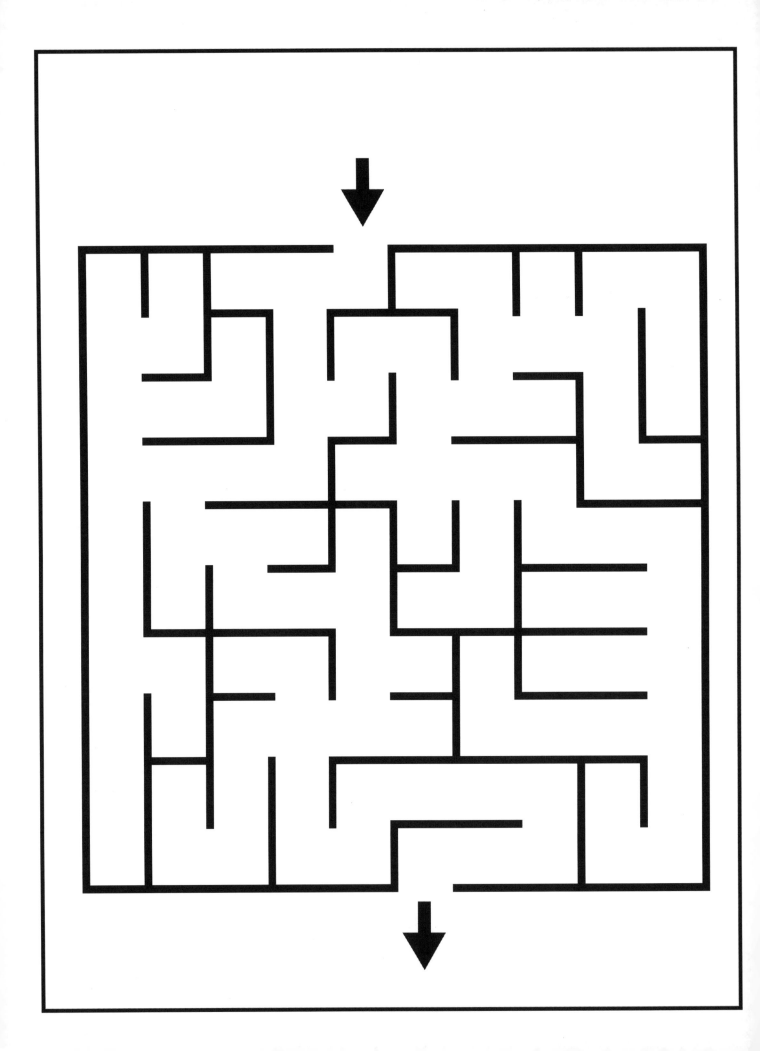

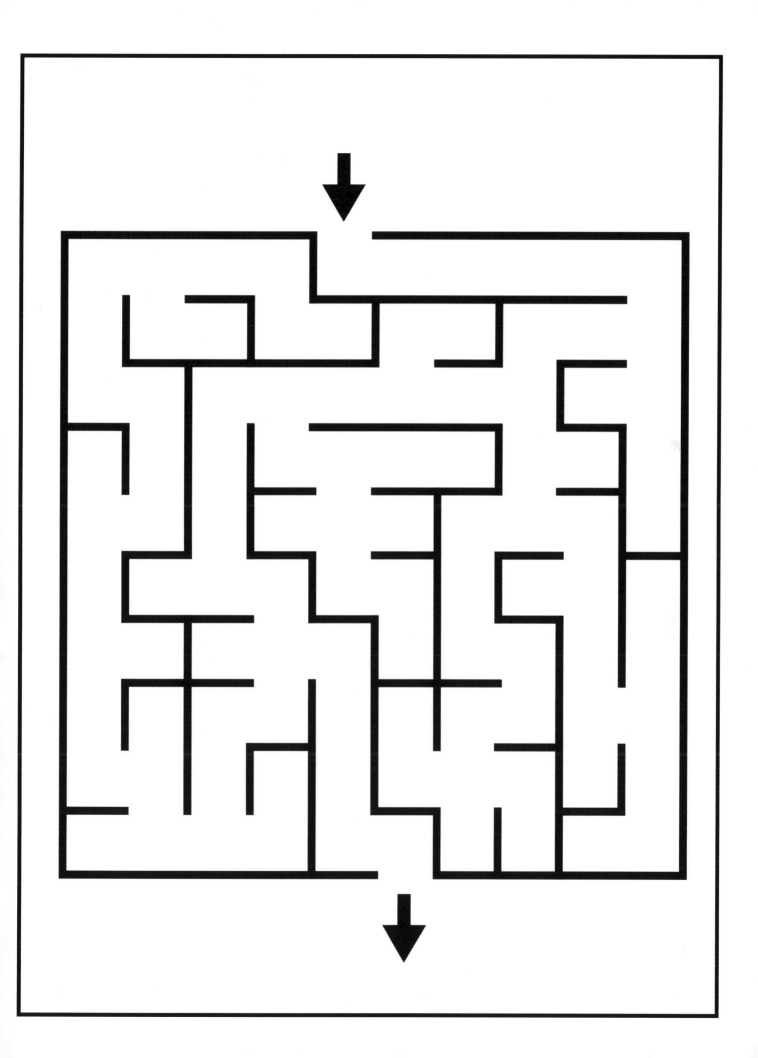

FIND ONE OF A KIND

FIND
ONE
OF A KIND

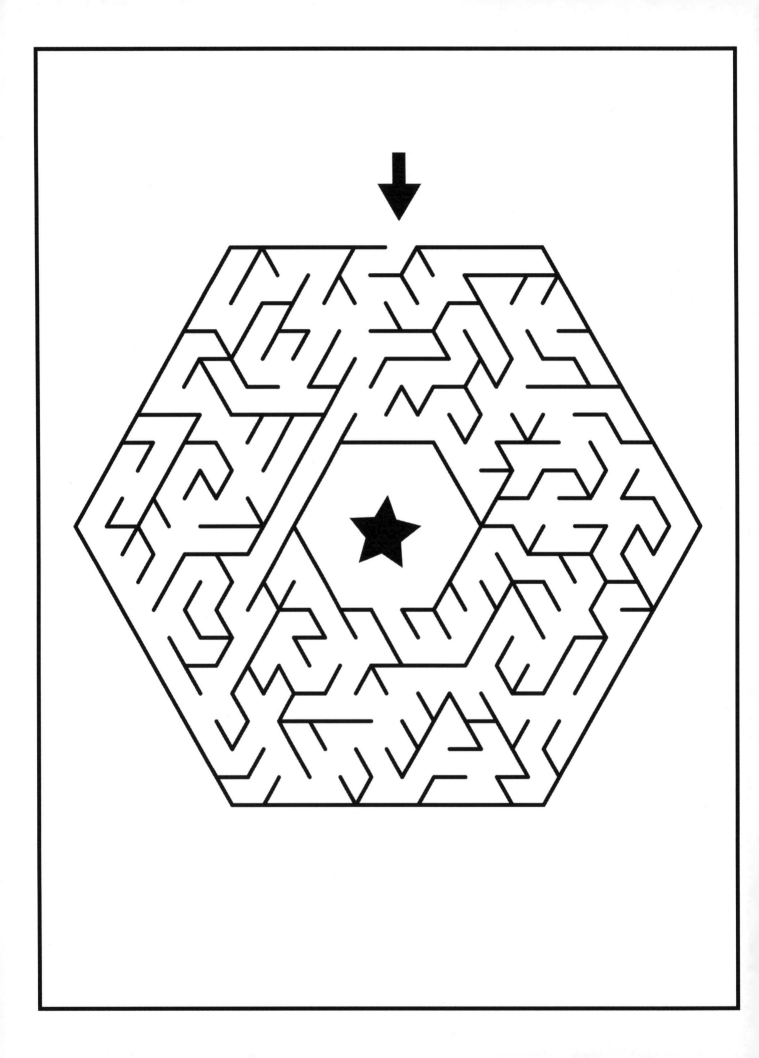

Find the ten differences between the two pictures.

# FIND TWO IDENTICAL PICTURES

# FIND TWO
# IDENTICAL
# PICTURES

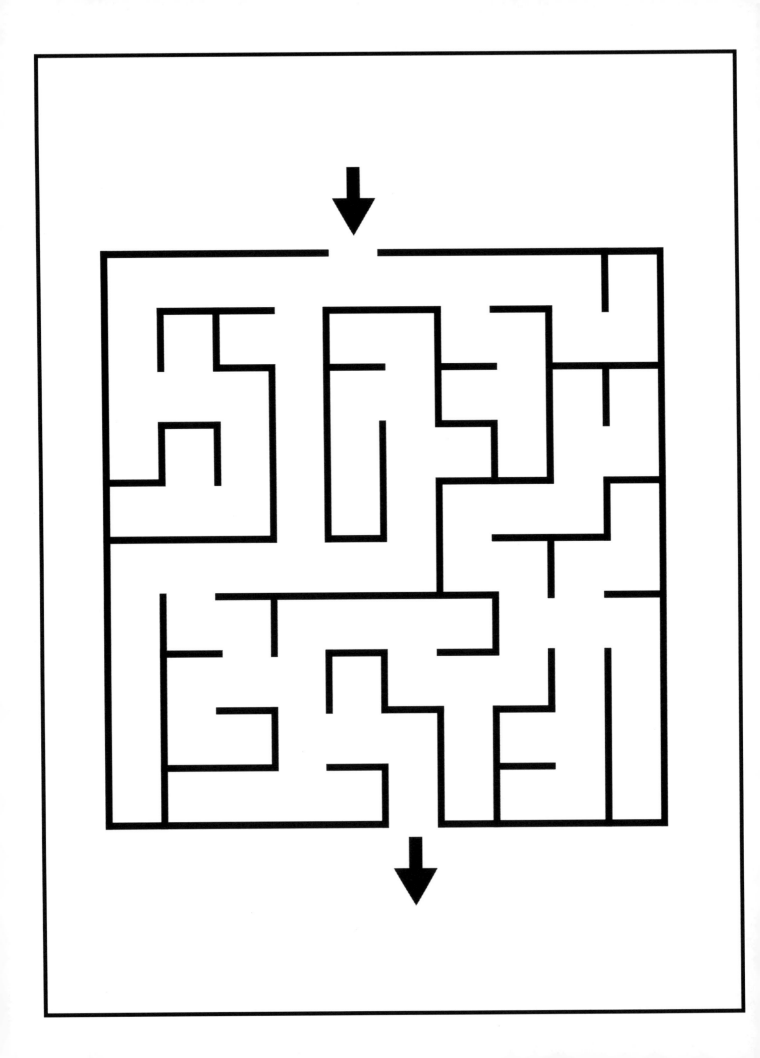

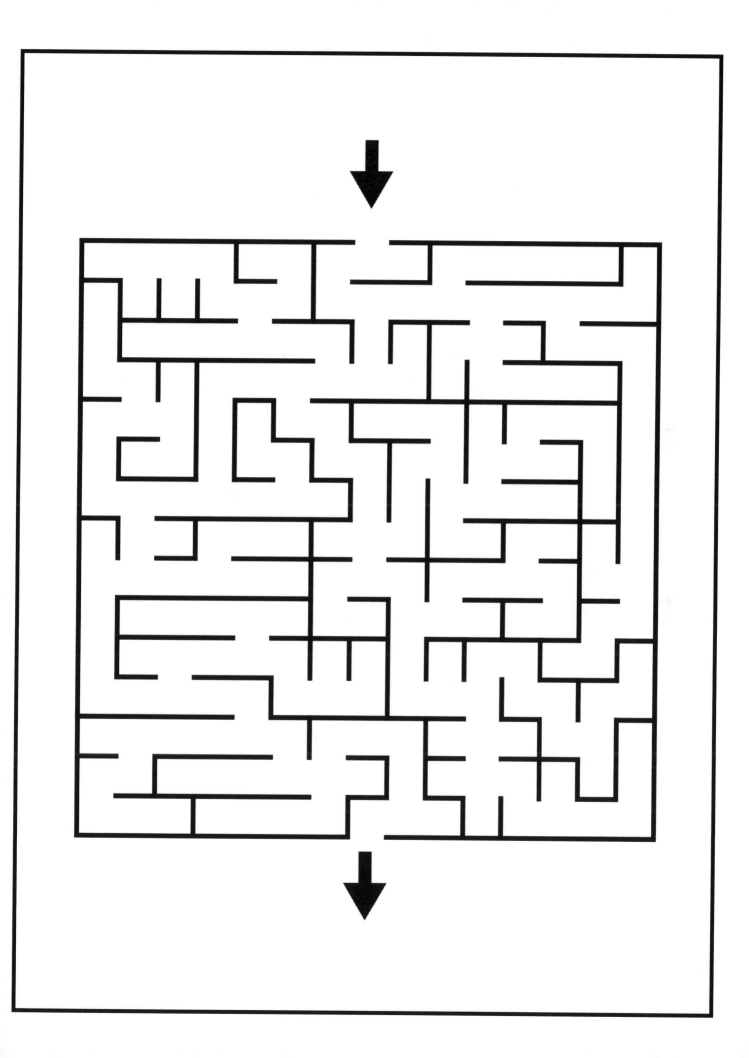

# DANCE

```
B  E  L  L  Y  Z  V  Q  F
B  F  O  X  T  R  O  T  Y
Q  A  D  B  O  T  Q  M  P
J  L  L  C  E  A  G  O  J
R  N  S  L  S  X  H  D  P
M  I  L  L  R  P  X  E  O
D  A  A  R  I  O  R  R  L
B  S  D  H  N  N  O  N  K
W  L  I  M  B  O  E  M  A
```

| | | |
|---|---|---|
| ballet | foxtrot | modern |
| ballroom | hiphop | polka |
| belly | limbo | salsa |
| disco | line | |

# ON THE FARM

```
C C R N Z G E Y J R H
Q O H L Z L K N K R Q
L B W I B U C K E T L
H F Z A C Y X K J E C
M A T J N K V J C T A
S S Y R C F E N F R T
H H O R S E E N A A T
E C N N K F Q W R C L
E B R C R O P S M T E
P A L H C J K P E O H
B R O O S T E R R R P
```

| barn | cow | horse |
|------|-----|-------|
| bucket | crops | rooster |
| cattle | farmer | sheep |
| chicken | fence | stable |
| corn | hay | tractor |

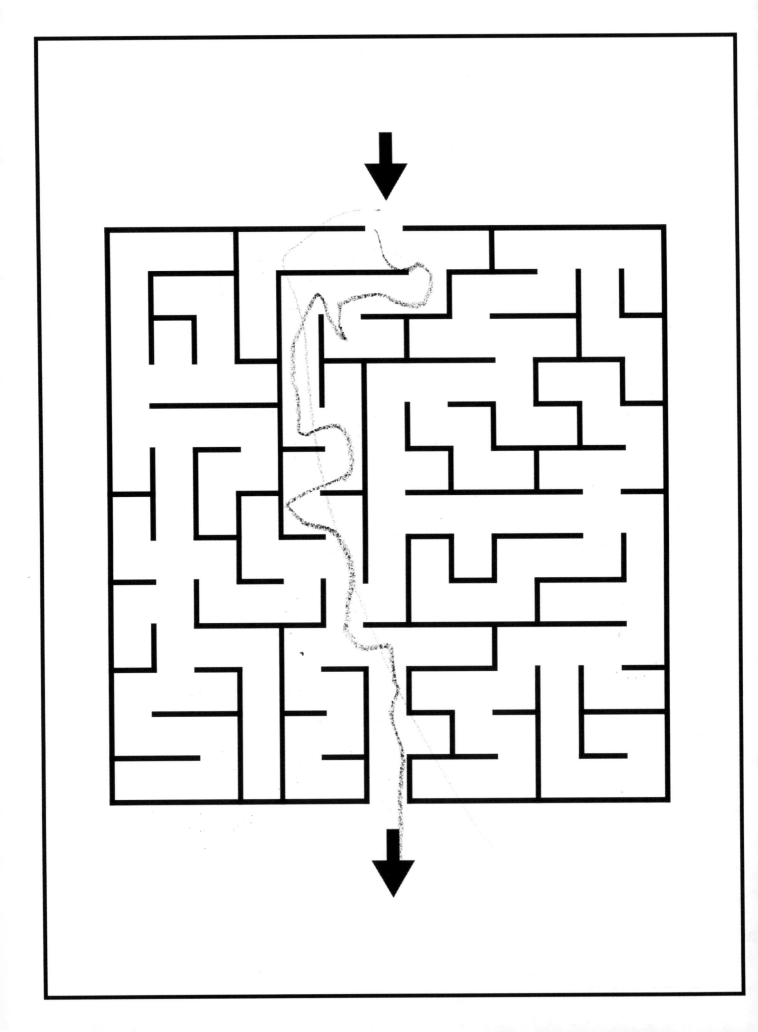

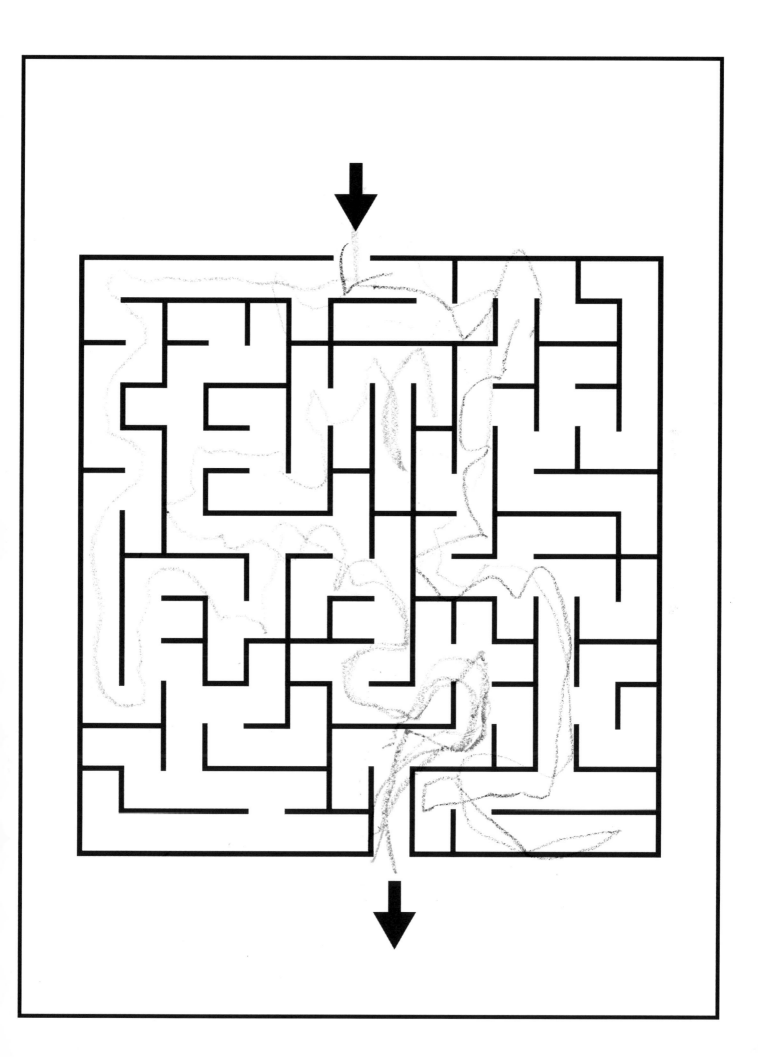

# FLOWERS

```
C  M  B  X  E  P  X  L  T  K  N
H  D  T  S  T  K  A  P  I  X  M
G  R  O  F  V  F  Y  N  N  L  K
N  R  Q  X  T  D  V  K  S  H  Y
G  M  A  R  I  G  O  L  D  Y  R
P  M  C  D  A  I  S  Y  D  A  Y
V  I  O  L  E  T  P  I  I  C  L
P  Z  M  K  T  I  H  N  R  W  I
F  F  Y  P  L  C  N  C  O  M  L
Y  C  J  U  R  I  M  L  S  P  A
B  L  T  O  Z  M  R  K  E  H  C
```

| daisy | orchid | tulip |
|-------|--------|-------|
| lilac | pansy | violet |
| lily | rose | zinnia |
| marigold | | |

# HIP HOP

```
B U L L F R O G H B
M A M P H I B I A N
T P O L L I W O G D
S A L A M A N D E R
Q H D K C Q D T F M
J W O P R N N L D P
D A L P O I N A M Q
B T J P A L O E H J
M E Y P K T E W W P
R R L P O I S O N T
```

amphibian          painted          tadpole

bullfrog           poison           toad

croak              polliwog         water

hop                pond

newt               salamander

# DOGS

```
Y  B  Q  H  Y  C  V  M  N  Q  H
L  N  E  J  Y  F  O  Q  B  N  C
A  N  B  A  R  K  B  R  B  M  H
B  H  F  T  G  P  O  D  G  F  I
R  P  U  D  E  L  X  R  W  I  H
A  Q  U  S  T  R  E  K  L  T  U
D  M  J  P  K  P  R  Q  D  A  A
O  N  R  X  P  Y  J  I  J  I  H
R  L  P  U  G  Y  K  H  E  L  U
G  R  E  Y  H  O  U  N  D  R  A
P  V  M  P  B  U  L  L  D  O  G
```

| | |
|---|---|
| bark | husky |
| beagle | labrador |
| boxer | pug |
| bulldog | puppy |
| chihuahua | tail |
| corgi | terrier |
| greyhound | |

# FRUIT

```
T Y S T R A W B E R R Y
Y N B L A C K B E R R Y
R O R G P E A R X H V B
R L Q N N P E V C K P R
E E N K R L C A A L I W
H M L G P C E K N M N N
C R E P R P H N A M E O
L E A L M A O D N L A R
N T X J O M P R A Q P A
M A N M E N L E B B P N
Y W R L N Q L N T L L G
B L U E B E R R Y L E E
```

Apple          Melon
Banana         Orange
Blackberry     Peach
Blueberry      Pear
Cherry         Pineapple
Grape          Strawberry
Lemon          Watermelon

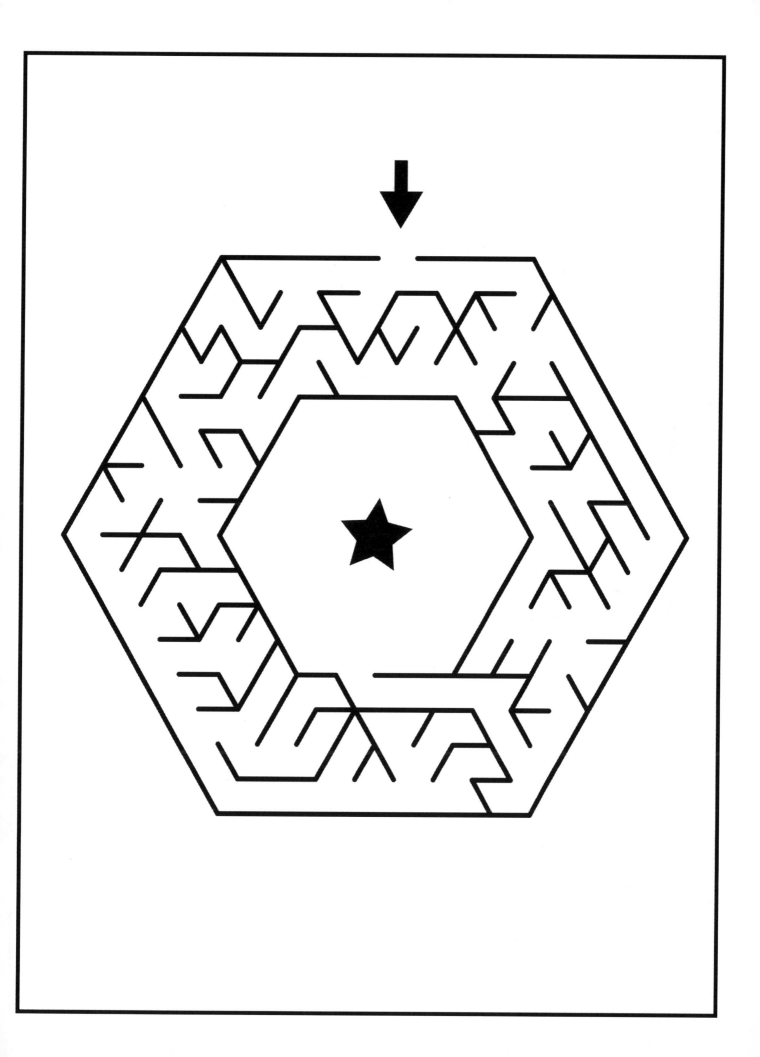

# FIND TWO IDENTICAL PICTURES

# FIND TWO
# IDENTICAL
# PICTURES

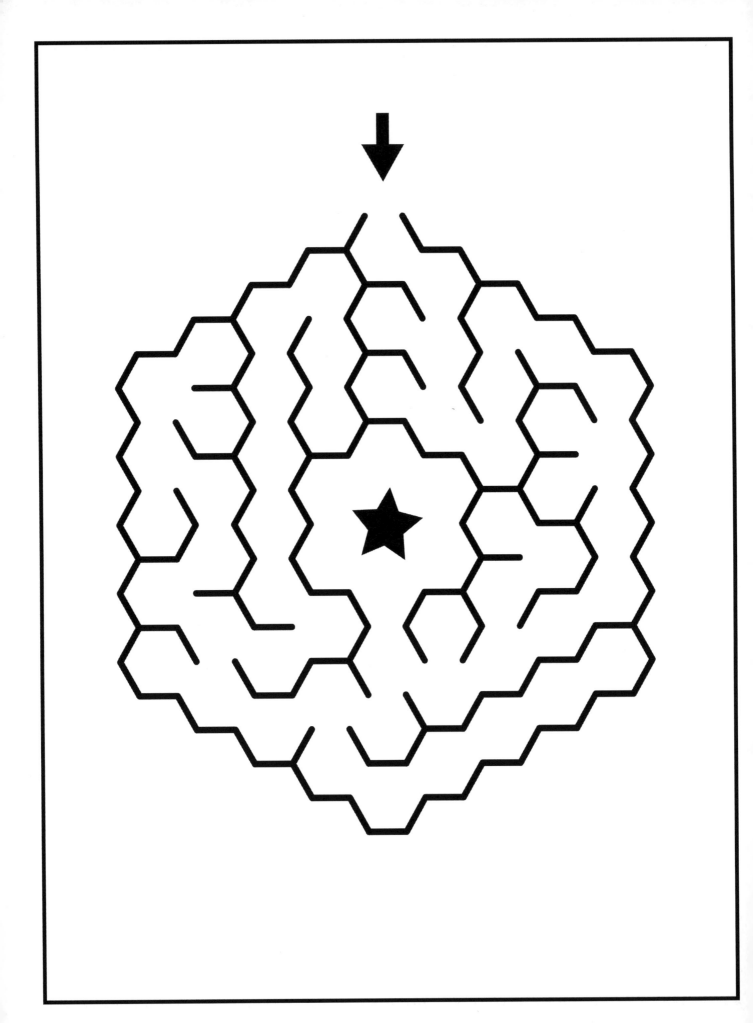

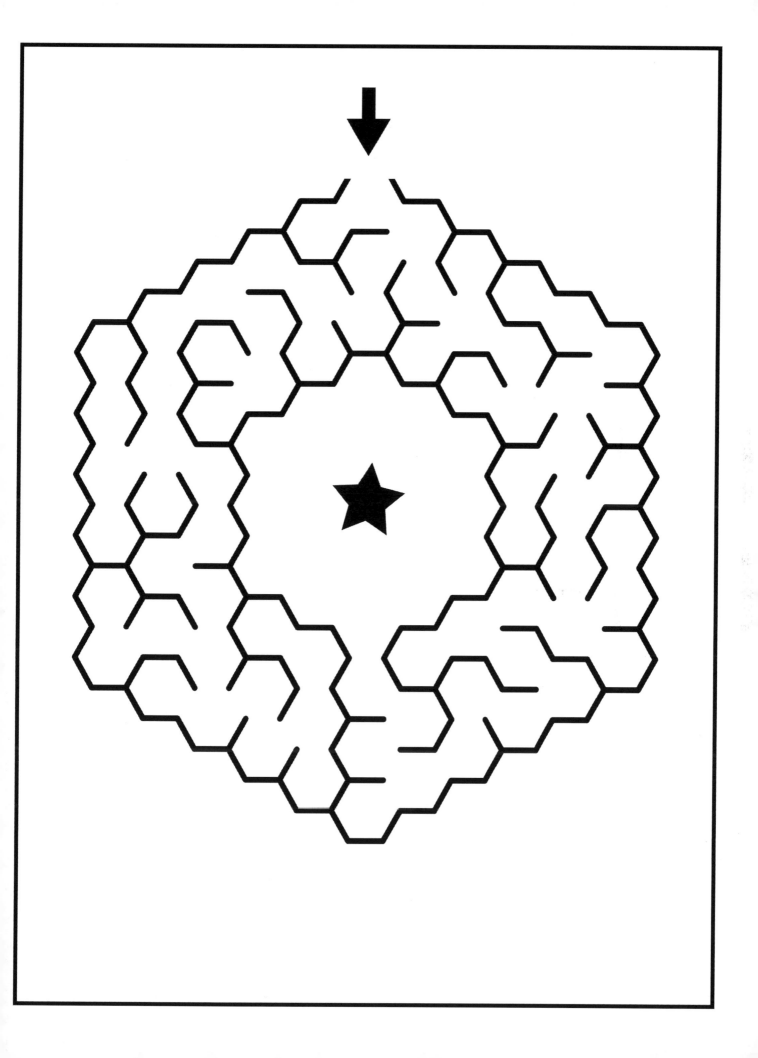

# FIRE FIGHTER

```
L  F  B  C  B  R  A  V  E  R  Y
C  J  L  Z  B  H  W  J  K  K  Y
O  H  A  A  C  V  A  X  E  C  F
N  Y  Z  R  M  A  R  D  S  X  O
T  D  E  F  S  E  P  T  V  Z  A
A  X  H  J  G  O  O  T  L  R  M
I  Q  Y  N  Y  O  N  T  A  M  G
N  V  A  K  B  W  X  X  R  I  G
Y  D  E  K  O  M  S  A  P  L  N
N  O  I  T  A  M  L  A  D  Q  Q
I  I  I  R  D  A  L  H  O  S  E
```

| alarm | bravery | drill |
|-------|---------|-------|
| arson | captain | flame |
| axe | contain | foam |
| blaze | dalmation | hose |
| boots | danger | smoke |

# SUMMER

L F R N B J Y Y K K
H T R F L N R S T L
Z P G I N X T L A M
T I T U S R Y H N K
H C S R O B C L Z N
U N M H I A E C T F
N I S L E P G E D W
D C N B Q K F B Y F
E K C A M P I N G H
R S U N S C R E E N

beach            shorts            thunder

camping          sunny             trip

frisbee          sunscreen

picnic           tan

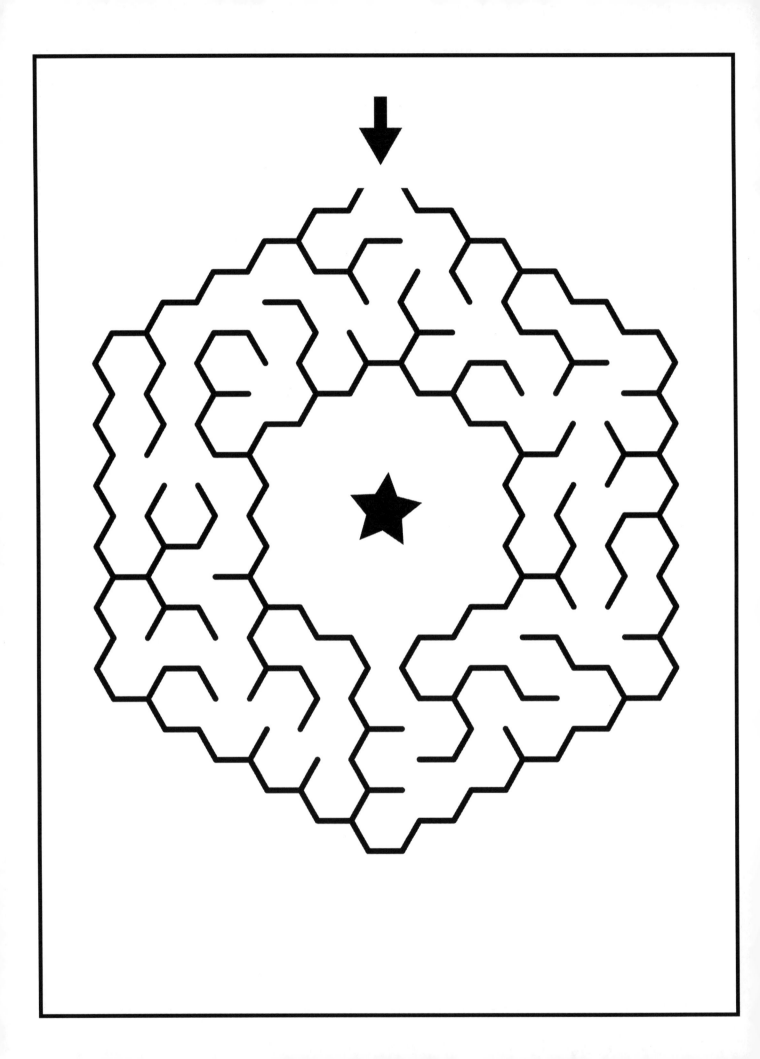

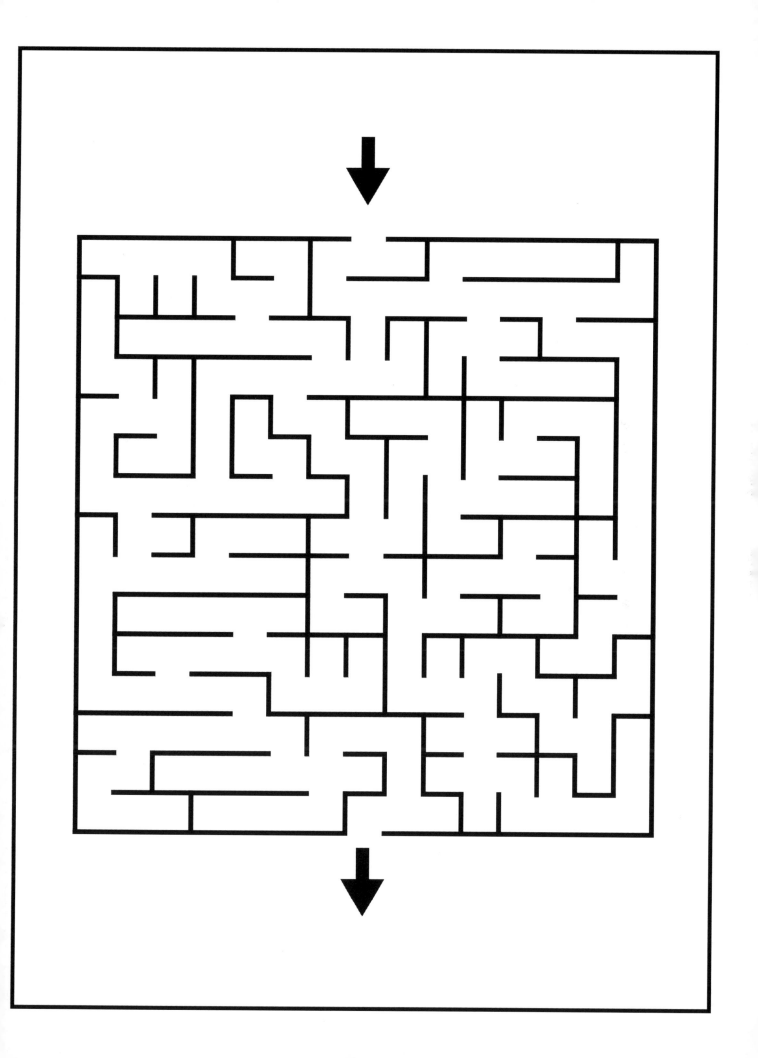

# SPANISH

```
F  S  N  B  U  R  R  O  F  A  X
L  A  W  L  N  N  T  C  T  R  N
O  L  D  L  A  I  C  S  A  M  A
R  S  C  I  U  S  E  H  L  P  C
I  A  T  Q  O  I  V  A  L  L  H
D  J  S  M  F  S  R  E  I  A  O
A  O  Z  W  L  R  P  D  G  Z  V
M  T  B  H  O  L  A  O  A  A  Z
T  L  K  C  K  J  C  V  T  X  S
W  T  D  R  C  A  R  G  O  W  M
R  B  B  T  T  L  P  Z  R  B  R
```

| ADIOS | FIESTA | NACHO |
|---|---|---|
| ALLIGATOR | FLORIDA | PLAZA |
| BURRO | HOLA | SALSA |
| CARGO | LASVEGAS | TACO |
| CORRAL | MOSQUITO | |

# SUPER

```
X  W  O  N  D  E  R  W  O  M  A  N  N
R  A  V  E  N  G  E  R  X  W  W  A  J
L  P  M  S  A  N  T  M  A  N  M  V  T
R  F  M  M  P  W  N  W  M  N  M  K  H
S  K  A  K  Y  I  R  R  O  F  N  H  O
B  U  F  L  V  K  D  R  D  Q  M  W  R
A  X  P  X  C  K  I  E  J  L  N  T  K
T  L  M  E  L  O  Y  L  R  Z  L  H  L
M  W  C  U  R  E  N  L  J  M  J  X  J
A  W  H  L  K  M  T  M  T  R  A  O  T
N  J  M  W  W  K  A  V  Y  Q  R  N  G
L  F  A  X  L  C  W  N  Q  E  R  R  Q
Q  H  M  L  P  M  L  Y  H  T  K  H  N
```

| antman | hawkeye | spiderman |
|--------|---------|-----------|
| avenger | hero | superman |
| batman | hulk | thor |
| falcon | ironman | wonderwoman |

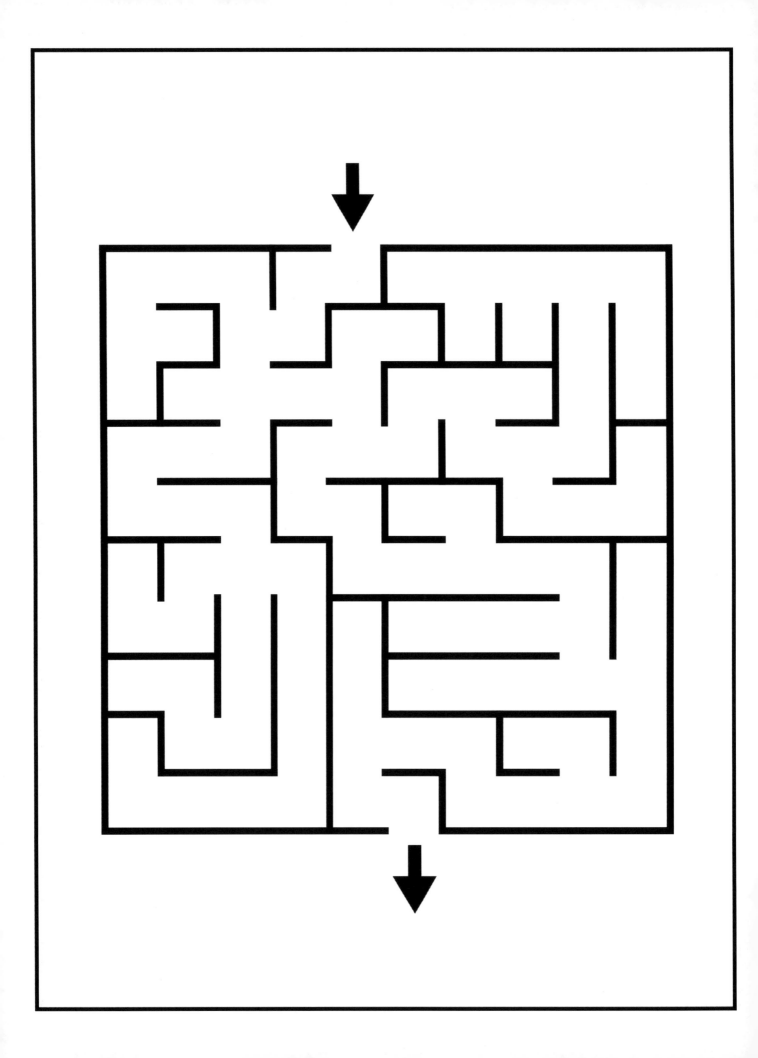

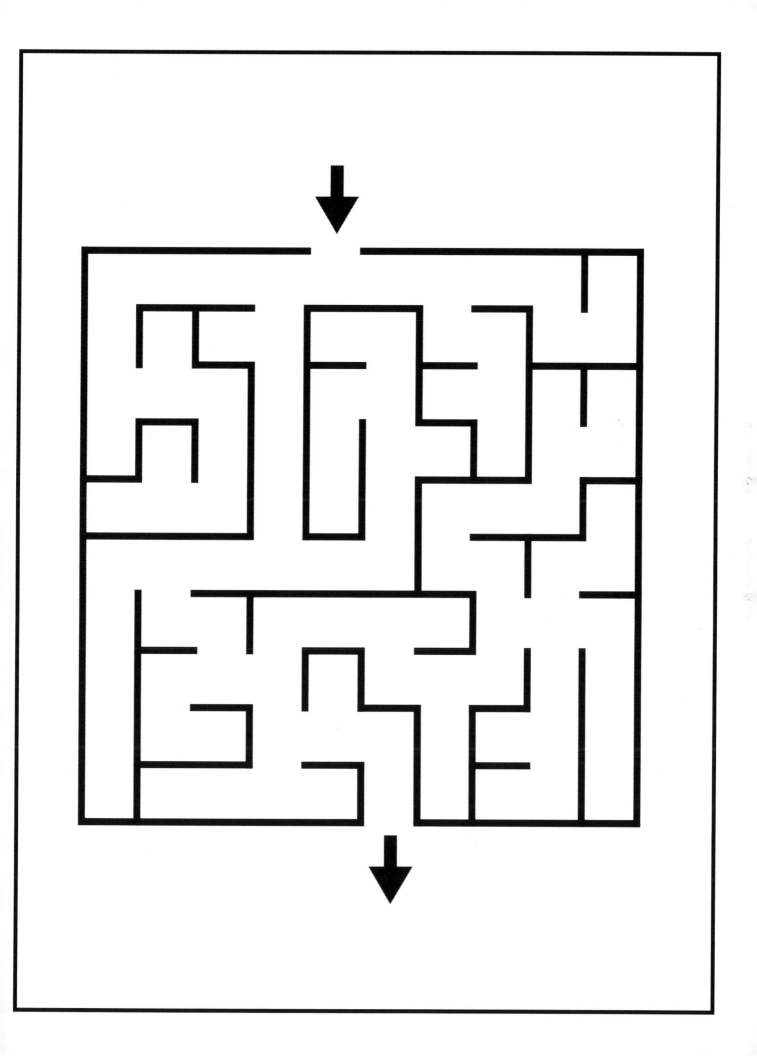

# BIG

```
T  M  T  R  A  I  N  N  Z  T  M
S  E  Q  U  O  I  A  T  N  R  A
M  C  W  A  L  K  E  L  T  E  N
Y  W  L  P  I  K  L  N  D  X  S
S  K  Y  S  C  R  A  P  E  R  I
Y  R  J  O  B  H  P  Z  E  B  O
T  M  R  J  P  Y  B  L  F  M  N
L  Z  M  E  N  N  A  L  A  Y  Z
F  R  L  Y  T  H  R  G  I  N  F
K  E  Y  M  W  C  K  Z  Z  M  E
S  T  A  D  I  U  M  F  X  N  P
```

AIRPLANE          ROCKET          TRAIN

BLIMP             SEQUOIA         TREX

ELEPHANT          SKYSCRAPER      WHALE

MANSION           STADIUM

# SPACE

```
T  P  X  X  D  N  M  M  X  N  V  Z
M  V  T  D  Q  P  L  A  N  E  T  N
T  E  L  E  S  C  O  P  E  H  O  Y
L  S  G  D  R  J  T  F  H  I  A  P
A  K  T  M  V  O  T  R  T  W  S  T
U  A  M  A  J  L  C  A  Y  P  T  D
N  H  L  Q  R  N  T  K  I  X  E  I
C  Q  D  I  O  S  L  H  E  G  R  P
H  T  J  O  E  I  S  C  C  T  O  P
M  B  M  M  M  N  P  X  K  K  I  E
Y  L  V  S  P  A  C  E  K  T  D  R
N  D  B  L  A  C  K  H  O  L  E  K
```

| | | |
|---|---|---|
| ALIEN | MILKYWAY | SPACE |
| ASTEROID | MOON | STARS |
| BLACKHOLE | PLANET | STATION |
| DIPPER | ROCKET | TELESCOPE |
| LAUNCH | SHIP | |

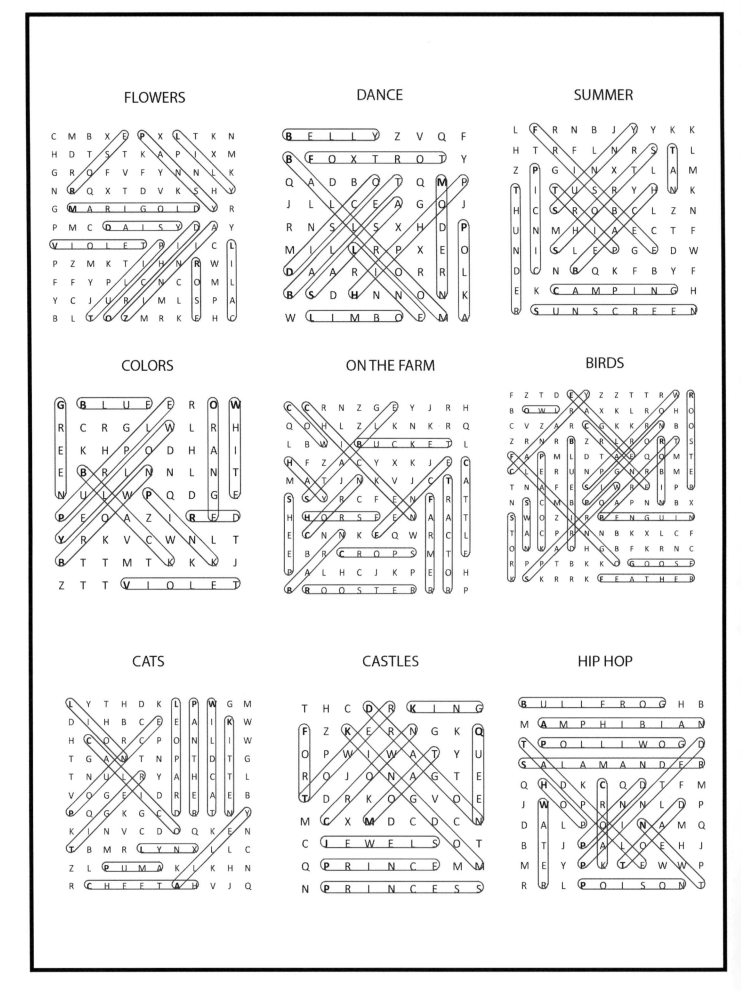

## FLOWERS

## DANCE

## SUMMER

## COLORS

## ON THE FARM

## BIRDS

## CATS

## CASTLES

## HIP HOP

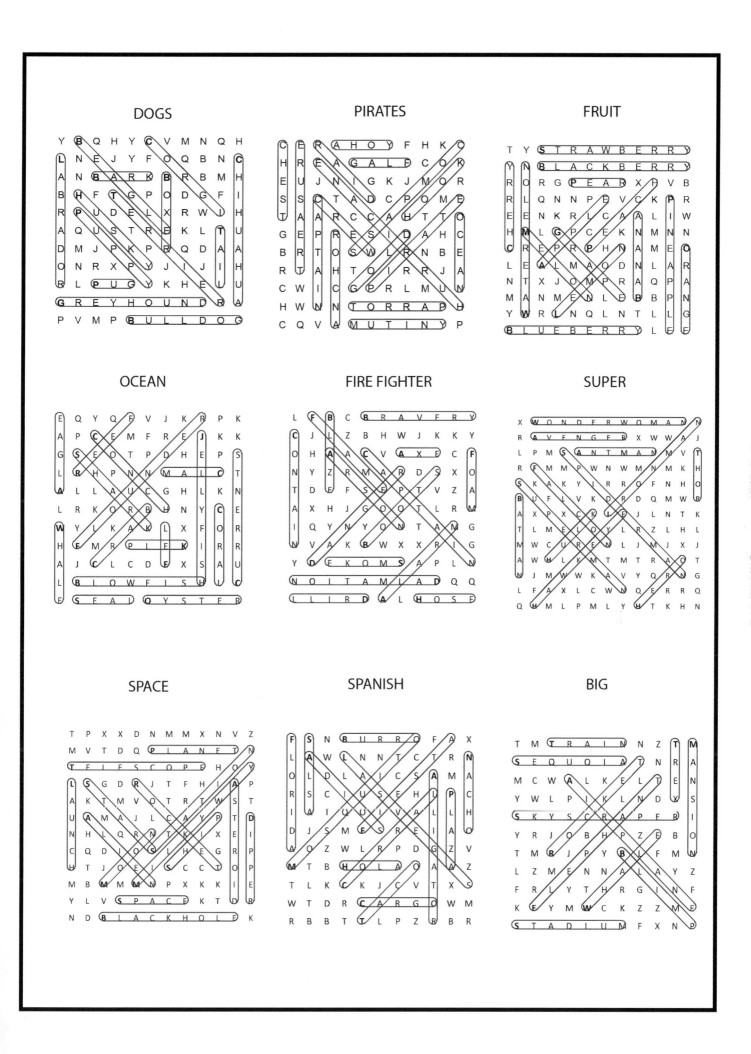

**FIND ONE OF A KIND**

**FIND ONE OF A KIND**

**FIND ONE OF A KIND**

**FIND ONE OF A KIND**

FIND TWO
IDENTICAL
PICTURES

FIND TWO
IDENTICAL
PICTURES

FIND TWO
IDENTICAL
PICTURES

FIND TWO
IDENTICAL
PICTURES

**Answers:**

Made in the USA
Columbia, SC
12 June 2021